This book belongs to

COFFEE NAME ______________________ DATE ____________

BEVERAGE ______________________

PLACE TASTED ______________________ PRICE ____________

COUNTRY / REGION ______________________

COMPANY ______________________

TESTING RATING

	0.5	1	1.5	2	2.5	3	3.5	4	4.5	5
APPEARANCE										
AROMA										
FLAVOR										

	0.5	1	1.5	2	2.5	3	3.5	4	4.5	5
SWEET										
ACIDIC										
SPICY										
CITRUS										
CHOCOLATE										
CARAMEL										
BITTER										
SAVORY										

BREW METHOD

DRIP ☐ ESPRESSO ☐ PRESS ☐

POUR-OVER ☐ SIPHON ☐ OTHER ________

NOTES

____

RECOMMEND TO

____

COFFEE NAME ______________ DATE ______________

BEVERAGE ______________

PLACE TASTED ______________ PRICE ______________

COUNTRY / REGION ______________

COMPANY ______________

TESTING RATING

	0.5	1	1.5	2	2.5	3	3.5	4	4.5	5
APPEARANCE										
AROMA										
FLAVOR										

	0.5	1	1.5	2	2.5	3	3.5	4	4.5	5
SWEET										
ACIDIC										
SPICY										
CITRUS										
CHOCOLATE										
CARAMEL										
BITTER										
SAVORY										

BREW METHOD

DRIP ☐ ESPRESSO ☐ PRESS ☐

POUR-OVER ☐ SIPHON ☐ OTHER ______

NOTES ______________

RECOMMEND TO ______________

COFFEE NAME ______________________ DATE ____________

BEVERAGE ______________________

PLACE TASTED ______________________ PRICE ____________

COUNTRY / REGION ______________________

COMPANY ______________________

TESTING RATING

	0.5	1	1.5	2	2.5	3	3.5	4	4.5	5
APPEARANCE										
AROMA										
FLAVOR										

	0.5	1	1.5	2	2.5	3	3.5	4	4.5	5
SWEET										
ACIDIC										
SPICY										
CITRUS										
CHOCOLATE										
CARAMEL										
BITTER										
SAVORY										

BREW METHOD

DRIP ☐ ESPRESSO ☐ PRESS ☐

POUR-OVER ☐ SIPHON ☐ OTHER ______

NOTES ______________________

RECOMMEND TO ______________________

COFFEE NAME ______________________ DATE ____________

BEVERAGE ______________________

PLACE TASTED ______________________ PRICE ____________

COUNTRY / REGION ______________________

COMPANY ______________________

TESTING RATING

	0.5	1	1.5	2	2.5	3	3.5	4	4.5	5
APPEARANCE										
AROMA										
FLAVOR										

	0.5	1	1.5	2	2.5	3	3.5	4	4.5	5
SWEET										
ACIDIC										
SPICY										
CITRUS										
CHOCOLATE										
CARAMEL										
BITTER										
SAVORY										

BREW METHOD

DRIP ☐ ESPRESSO ☐ PRESS ☐

POUR-OVER ☐ SIPHON ☐ OTHER ________

NOTES ______________________

RECOMMEND TO ______________________

COFFEE NAME ______________________ DATE ____________

BEVERAGE ______________________

PLACE TASTED ______________________ PRICE ____________

COUNTRY / REGION ______________________

COMPANY ______________________

TESTING RATING

	0.5	1	1.5	2	2.5	3	3.5	4	4.5	5
APPEARANCE										
AROMA										
FLAVOR										

	0.5	1	1.5	2	2.5	3	3.5	4	4.5	5
SWEET										
ACIDIC										
SPICY										
CITRUS										
CHOCOLATE										
CARAMEL										
BITTER										
SAVORY										

BREW METHOD

DRIP ☐ ESPRESSO ☐ PRESS ☐

POUR-OVER ☐ SIPHON ☐ OTHER ______

NOTES ______________________

RECOMMEND TO ______________________

COFFEE NAME ________________________ DATE ____________

BEVERAGE ________________________

PLACE TASTED ________________________ PRICE ____________

COUNTRY / REGION ____________________

COMPANY ________________________

TESTING RATING

	0.5	1	1.5	2	2.5	3	3.5	4	4.5	5
APPEARANCE										
AROMA										
FLAVOR										

	0.5	1	1.5	2	2.5	3	3.5	4	4.5	5
SWEET										
ACIDIC										
SPICY										
CITRUS										
CHOCOLATE										
CARAMEL										
BITTER										
SAVORY										

BREW METHOD

DRIP ☐ ESPRESSO ☐ PRESS ☐

POUR-OVER ☐ SIPHON ☐ OTHER ________

NOTES

RECOMMEND TO

COFFEE NAME ______________ DATE ________

BEVERAGE ______________

PLACE TASTED ______________ PRICE ________

COUNTRY / REGION ______________

COMPANY ______________

TESTING RATING

	0.5	1	1.5	2	2.5	3	3.5	4	4.5	5
APPEARANCE										
AROMA										
FLAVOR										

	0.5	1	1.5	2	2.5	3	3.5	4	4.5	5
SWEET										
ACIDIC										
SPICY										
CITRUS										
CHOCOLATE										
CARAMEL										
BITTER										
SAVORY										

BREW METHOD

DRIP ☐ ESPRESSO ☐ PRESS ☐

POUR-OVER ☐ SIPHON ☐ OTHER ________

NOTES

RECOMMEND TO

COFFEE NAME ____________________ DATE ____________

BEVERAGE ____________________

PLACE TASTED ____________________ PRICE ____________

COUNTRY / REGION ____________________

COMPANY ____________________

TESTING RATING

	0.5	1	1.5	2	2.5	3	3.5	4	4.5	5
APPEARANCE										
AROMA										
FLAVOR										

	0.5	1	1.5	2	2.5	3	3.5	4	4.5	5
SWEET										
ACIDIC										
SPICY										
CITRUS										
CHOCOLATE										
CARAMEL										
BITTER										
SAVORY										

BREW METHOD

DRIP ☐ ESPRESSO ☐ PRESS ☐

POUR-OVER ☐ SIPHON ☐ OTHER ________

NOTES ____________________

RECOMMEND TO ____________________

COFFEE NAME ______________________ DATE ____________

BEVERAGE ______________________

PLACE TASTED ______________________ PRICE ____________

COUNTRY / REGION ______________________

COMPANY ______________________

TESTING RATING

	0.5	1	1.5	2	2.5	3	3.5	4	4.5	5
APPEARANCE										
AROMA										
FLAVOR										

	0.5	1	1.5	2	2.5	3	3.5	4	4.5	5
SWEET										
ACIDIC										
SPICY										
CITRUS										
CHOCOLATE										
CARAMEL										
BITTER										
SAVORY										

BREW METHOD

DRIP ☐ ESPRESSO ☐ PRESS ☐

POUR-OVER ☐ SIPHON ☐ OTHER ________

NOTES ______________________

RECOMMEND TO ______________________

COFFEE NAME ______________________ DATE ____________

BEVERAGE ______________________

PLACE TASTED ______________________ PRICE ____________

COUNTRY / REGION ______________________

COMPANY ______________________

TESTING RATING

	0.5	1	1.5	2	2.5	3	3.5	4	4.5	5
APPEARANCE										
AROMA										
FLAVOR										

	0.5	1	1.5	2	2.5	3	3.5	4	4.5	5
SWEET										
ACIDIC										
SPICY										
CITRUS										
CHOCOLATE										
CARAMEL										
BITTER										
SAVORY										

BREW METHOD

DRIP ☐ ESPRESSO ☐ PRESS ☐

POUR-OVER ☐ SIPHON ☐ OTHER ________

NOTES

RECOMMEND TO

COFFEE NAME ______________________ DATE ____________

BEVERAGE ______________________

PLACE TASTED ______________________ PRICE ____________

COUNTRY / REGION ______________________

COMPANY ______________________

TESTING RATING

	0.5	1	1.5	2	2.5	3	3.5	4	4.5	5
APPEARANCE										
AROMA										
FLAVOR										

	0.5	1	1.5	2	2.5	3	3.5	4	4.5	5
SWEET										
ACIDIC										
SPICY										
CITRUS										
CHOCOLATE										
CARAMEL										
BITTER										
SAVORY										

BREW METHOD

DRIP ☐ ESPRESSO ☐ PRESS ☐

POUR-OVER ☐ SIPHON ☐ OTHER ________

NOTES ______________________

RECOMMEND TO ______________________

COFFEE NAME ______________________ DATE ____________

BEVERAGE ______________________

PLACE TASTED ______________________ PRICE ____________

COUNTRY / REGION ______________________

COMPANY ______________________

TESTING RATING

	0.5	1	1.5	2	2.5	3	3.5	4	4.5	5
APPEARANCE										
AROMA										
FLAVOR										

	0.5	1	1.5	2	2.5	3	3.5	4	4.5	5
SWEET										
ACIDIC										
SPICY										
CITRUS										
CHOCOLATE										
CARAMEL										
BITTER										
SAVORY										

BREW METHOD

DRIP ☐ ESPRESSO ☐ PRESS ☐

POUR-OVER ☐ SIPHON ☐ OTHER ________

NOTES ______________________

RECOMMEND TO ______________________

COFFEE NAME ______________________ DATE ____________

BEVERAGE ______________________

PLACE TASTED ______________________ PRICE ____________

COUNTRY / REGION ______________________

COMPANY ______________________

TESTING RATING

	0.5	1	1.5	2	2.5	3	3.5	4	4.5	5
APPEARANCE										
AROMA										
FLAVOR										

	0.5	1	1.5	2	2.5	3	3.5	4	4.5	5
SWEET										
ACIDIC										
SPICY										
CITRUS										
CHOCOLATE										
CARAMEL										
BITTER										
SAVORY										

BREW METHOD

DRIP ☐ ESPRESSO ☐ PRESS ☐

POUR-OVER ☐ SIPHON ☐ OTHER ________

NOTES

RECOMMEND TO

COFFEE NAME ______________________ DATE ____________

BEVERAGE ______________________

PLACE TASTED ______________________ PRICE ____________

COUNTRY / REGION ______________________

COMPANY ______________________

TESTING RATING

	0.5	1	1.5	2	2.5	3	3.5	4	4.5	5
APPEARANCE										
AROMA										
FLAVOR										

	0.5	1	1.5	2	2.5	3	3.5	4	4.5	5
SWEET										
ACIDIC										
SPICY										
CITRUS										
CHOCOLATE										
CARAMEL										
BITTER										
SAVORY										

BREW METHOD

DRIP ☐ ESPRESSO ☐ PRESS ☐

POUR-OVER ☐ SIPHON ☐ OTHER ______

NOTES ______________________

RECOMMEND TO ______________________

COFFEE NAME ______________________ DATE ____________

BEVERAGE ______________________

PLACE TASTED ______________________ PRICE ____________

COUNTRY / REGION ______________________

COMPANY ______________________

TESTING RATING

	0.5	1	1.5	2	2.5	3	3.5	4	4.5	5
APPEARANCE										
AROMA										
FLAVOR										

	0.5	1	1.5	2	2.5	3	3.5	4	4.5	5
SWEET										
ACIDIC										
SPICY										
CITRUS										
CHOCOLATE										
CARAMEL										
BITTER										
SAVORY										

BREW METHOD

DRIP ☐ ESPRESSO ☐ PRESS ☐

POUR-OVER ☐ SIPHON ☐ OTHER ________

NOTES ______________________

RECOMMEND TO ______________________

COFFEE NAME ______________________ DATE ____________

BEVERAGE ______________________

PLACE TASTED ______________________ PRICE ____________

COUNTRY / REGION ______________________

COMPANY ______________________

TESTING RATING

	0.5	1	1.5	2	2.5	3	3.5	4	4.5	5
APPEARANCE										
AROMA										
FLAVOR										

BREW METHOD

DRIP ☐ ESPRESSO ☐ PRESS ☐

POUR-OVER ☐ SIPHON ☐ OTHER ________

	0.5	1	1.5	2	2.5	3	3.5	4	4.5	5
SWEET										
ACIDIC										
SPICY										
CITRUS										
CHOCOLATE										
CARAMEL										
BITTER										
SAVORY										

NOTES

RECOMMEND TO

COFFEE NAME ______________________ DATE ____________

BEVERAGE ______________________

PLACE TASTED ______________________ PRICE ____________

COUNTRY / REGION ______________________

COMPANY ______________________

TESTING RATING

	0.5	1	1.5	2	2.5	3	3.5	4	4.5	5
APPEARANCE										
AROMA										
FLAVOR										

	0.5	1	1.5	2	2.5	3	3.5	4	4.5	5
SWEET										
ACIDIC										
SPICY										
CITRUS										
CHOCOLATE										
CARAMEL										
BITTER										
SAVORY										

BREW METHOD

DRIP ☐ ESPRESSO ☐ PRESS ☐

POUR-OVER ☐ SIPHON ☐ OTHER ________

NOTES

RECOMMEND TO

COFFEE NAME ______________________ DATE ____________

BEVERAGE ______________________

PLACE TASTED ______________________ PRICE ____________

COUNTRY / REGION ______________________

COMPANY ______________________

TESTING RATING

	0.5	1	1.5	2	2.5	3	3.5	4	4.5	5
APPEARANCE										
AROMA										
FLAVOR										

	0.5	1	1.5	2	2.5	3	3.5	4	4.5	5
SWEET										
ACIDIC										
SPICY										
CITRUS										
CHOCOLATE										
CARAMEL										
BITTER										
SAVORY										

BREW METHOD

DRIP ☐ ESPRESSO ☐ PRESS ☐

POUR-OVER ☐ SIPHON ☐ OTHER ________

NOTES ______________________

RECOMMEND TO ______________________

COFFEE NAME ______________________ DATE ____________

BEVERAGE ______________________

PLACE TASTED ______________________ PRICE ____________

COUNTRY / REGION ______________________

COMPANY ______________________

TESTING RATING

	0.5	1	1.5	2	2.5	3	3.5	4	4.5	5
APPEARANCE										
AROMA										
FLAVOR										

	0.5	1	1.5	2	2.5	3	3.5	4	4.5	5
SWEET										
ACIDIC										
SPICY										
CITRUS										
CHOCOLATE										
CARAMEL										
BITTER										
SAVORY										

BREW METHOD

DRIP ☐ ESPRESSO ☐ PRESS ☐

POUR-OVER ☐ SIPHON ☐ OTHER ________

NOTES ______________________

RECOMMEND TO ______________________

COFFEE NAME ____________ DATE ____________

BEVERAGE ____________

PLACE TASTED ____________ PRICE ____________

COUNTRY / REGION ____________

COMPANY ____________

TESTING RATING

	0.5	1	1.5	2	2.5	3	3.5	4	4.5	5
APPEARANCE										
AROMA										
FLAVOR										

	0.5	1	1.5	2	2.5	3	3.5	4	4.5	5
SWEET										
ACIDIC										
SPICY										
CITRUS										
CHOCOLATE										
CARAMEL										
BITTER										
SAVORY										

BREW METHOD

DRIP ☐ ESPRESSO ☐ PRESS ☐

POUR-OVER ☐ SIPHON ☐ OTHER ______

NOTES

RECOMMEND TO

COFFEE NAME ______________________ DATE ____________

BEVERAGE ______________________

PLACE TASTED ______________________ PRICE ____________

COUNTRY / REGION ______________________

COMPANY ______________________

TESTING RATING

	0.5	1	1.5	2	2.5	3	3.5	4	4.5	5
APPEARANCE										
AROMA										
FLAVOR										

BREW METHOD

DRIP ☐ ESPRESSO ☐ PRESS ☐

POUR-OVER ☐ SIPHON ☐ OTHER ________

	0.5	1	1.5	2	2.5	3	3.5	4	4.5	5
SWEET										
ACIDIC										
SPICY										
CITRUS										
CHOCOLATE										
CARAMEL										
BITTER										
SAVORY										

NOTES

RECOMMEND TO

COFFEE NAME ______________________ DATE ____________

BEVERAGE ______________________

PLACE TASTED ______________________ PRICE ____________

COUNTRY / REGION ______________________

COMPANY ______________________

TESTING RATING

	0.5	1	1.5	2	2.5	3	3.5	4	4.5	5
APPEARANCE										
AROMA										
FLAVOR										

	0.5	1	1.5	2	2.5	3	3.5	4	4.5	5
SWEET										
ACIDIC										
SPICY										
CITRUS										
CHOCOLATE										
CARAMEL										
BITTER										
SAVORY										

BREW METHOD

DRIP ☐ ESPRESSO ☐ PRESS ☐

POUR-OVER ☐ SIPHON ☐ OTHER ______

NOTES ______________________

RECOMMEND TO ______________________

COFFEE NAME ______________________ DATE ____________

BEVERAGE ______________________

PLACE TASTED ______________________ PRICE ____________

COUNTRY / REGION ______________________

COMPANY ______________________

TESTING RATING

	0.5	1	1.5	2	2.5	3	3.5	4	4.5	5
APPEARANCE										
AROMA										
FLAVOR										

	0.5	1	1.5	2	2.5	3	3.5	4	4.5	5
SWEET										
ACIDIC										
SPICY										
CITRUS										
CHOCOLATE										
CARAMEL										
BITTER										
SAVORY										

BREW METHOD

DRIP ☐ ESPRESSO ☐ PRESS ☐

POUR-OVER ☐ SIPHON ☐ OTHER ________

NOTES

____

RECOMMEND TO

____

COFFEE NAME ______________________ DATE ____________

BEVERAGE ______________________

PLACE TASTED ______________________ PRICE ____________

COUNTRY / REGION ______________________

COMPANY ______________________

TESTING RATING

	0.5	1	1.5	2	2.5	3	3.5	4	4.5	5
APPEARANCE										
AROMA										
FLAVOR										

	0.5	1	1.5	2	2.5	3	3.5	4	4.5	5
SWEET										
ACIDIC										
SPICY										
CITRUS										
CHOCOLATE										
CARAMEL										
BITTER										
SAVORY										

BREW METHOD

DRIP ☐ ESPRESSO ☐ PRESS ☐

POUR-OVER ☐ SIPHON ☐ OTHER ______

NOTES

RECOMMEND TO

COFFEE NAME ______________________ DATE ____________

BEVERAGE ______________________

PLACE TASTED ______________________ PRICE ____________

COUNTRY / REGION ______________________

COMPANY ______________________

TESTING RATING

	0.5	1	1.5	2	2.5	3	3.5	4	4.5	5
APPEARANCE										
AROMA										
FLAVOR										

	0.5	1	1.5	2	2.5	3	3.5	4	4.5	5
SWEET										
ACIDIC										
SPICY										
CITRUS										
CHOCOLATE										
CARAMEL										
BITTER										
SAVORY										

BREW METHOD

DRIP ☐ ESPRESSO ☐ PRESS ☐

POUR-OVER ☐ SIPHON ☐ OTHER ________

NOTES

____

RECOMMEND TO

____

COFFEE NAME ______________________ DATE ____________

BEVERAGE ______________________

PLACE TASTED ______________________ PRICE ____________

COUNTRY / REGION ______________________

COMPANY ______________________

TESTING RATING

	0.5	1	1.5	2	2.5	3	3.5	4	4.5	5
APPEARANCE										
AROMA										
FLAVOR										

	0.5	1	1.5	2	2.5	3	3.5	4	4.5	5
SWEET										
ACIDIC										
SPICY										
CITRUS										
CHOCOLATE										
CARAMEL										
BITTER										
SAVORY										

BREW METHOD

DRIP ☐ ESPRESSO ☐ PRESS ☐

POUR-OVER ☐ SIPHON ☐ OTHER ________

NOTES ______________________

RECOMMEND TO ______________________

COFFEE NAME ______________________ DATE ____________

BEVERAGE ______________________

PLACE TASTED ______________________ PRICE ____________

COUNTRY / REGION ______________________

COMPANY ______________________

TESTING RATING

	0.5	1	1.5	2	2.5	3	3.5	4	4.5	5
APPEARANCE										
AROMA										
FLAVOR										

BREW METHOD

DRIP ☐ ESPRESSO ☐ PRESS ☐

POUR-OVER ☐ SIPHON ☐ OTHER ________

	0.5	1	1.5	2	2.5	3	3.5	4	4.5	5
SWEET										
ACIDIC										
SPICY										
CITRUS										
CHOCOLATE										
CARAMEL										
BITTER										
SAVORY										

NOTES ______________________

RECOMMEND TO ______________________

COFFEE NAME ________________ DATE ________

BEVERAGE ________________

PLACE TASTED ________________ PRICE ________

COUNTRY / REGION ________________

COMPANY ________________

TESTING RATING

	0.5	1	1.5	2	2.5	3	3.5	4	4.5	5
APPEARANCE										
AROMA										
FLAVOR										

	0.5	1	1.5	2	2.5	3	3.5	4	4.5	5
SWEET										
ACIDIC										
SPICY										
CITRUS										
CHOCOLATE										
CARAMEL										
BITTER										
SAVORY										

BREW METHOD

DRIP ☐ ESPRESSO ☐ PRESS ☐

POUR-OVER ☐ SIPHON ☐ OTHER ________

NOTES ________________

RECOMMEND TO ________________

COFFEE NAME ______________________ DATE ____________

BEVERAGE ______________________

PLACE TASTED ______________________ PRICE ____________

COUNTRY / REGION ______________________

COMPANY ______________________

TESTING RATING

	0.5	1	1.5	2	2.5	3	3.5	4	4.5	5
APPEARANCE										
AROMA										
FLAVOR										

	0.5	1	1.5	2	2.5	3	3.5	4	4.5	5
SWEET										
ACIDIC										
SPICY										
CITRUS										
CHOCOLATE										
CARAMEL										
BITTER										
SAVORY										

BREW METHOD

DRIP ☐ ESPRESSO ☐ PRESS ☐

POUR-OVER ☐ SIPHON ☐ OTHER ________

NOTES ______________________

RECOMMEND TO ______________________

COFFEE NAME ______________________ DATE ____________

BEVERAGE ______________________

PLACE TASTED ______________________ PRICE ____________

COUNTRY / REGION ______________________

COMPANY ______________________

TESTING RATING

	0.5	1	1.5	2	2.5	3	3.5	4	4.5	5
APPEARANCE										
AROMA										
FLAVOR										

	0.5	1	1.5	2	2.5	3	3.5	4	4.5	5
SWEET										
ACIDIC										
SPICY										
CITRUS										
CHOCOLATE										
CARAMEL										
BITTER										
SAVORY										

BREW METHOD

DRIP ☐ ESPRESSO ☐ PRESS ☐

POUR-OVER ☐ SIPHON ☐ OTHER ______

NOTES ______________________

RECOMMEND TO ______________________

COFFEE NAME ______________________ DATE ____________

BEVERAGE ______________________

PLACE TASTED ______________________ PRICE ____________

COUNTRY / REGION ______________________

COMPANY ______________________

TESTING RATING

	0.5	1	1.5	2	2.5	3	3.5	4	4.5	5
APPEARANCE										
AROMA										
FLAVOR										

	0.5	1	1.5	2	2.5	3	3.5	4	4.5	5
SWEET										
ACIDIC										
SPICY										
CITRUS										
CHOCOLATE										
CARAMEL										
BITTER										
SAVORY										

BREW METHOD

DRIP ☐ ESPRESSO ☐ PRESS ☐

POUR-OVER ☐ SIPHON ☐ OTHER ________

NOTES ______________________

RECOMMEND TO ______________________

COFFEE NAME ____________ DATE ____________

BEVERAGE ____________

PLACE TASTED ____________ PRICE ____________

COUNTRY / REGION ____________

COMPANY ____________

TESTING RATING

	0.5	1	1.5	2	2.5	3	3.5	4	4.5	5
APPEARANCE										
AROMA										
FLAVOR										

	0.5	1	1.5	2	2.5	3	3.5	4	4.5	5
SWEET										
ACIDIC										
SPICY										
CITRUS										
CHOCOLATE										
CARAMEL										
BITTER										
SAVORY										

BREW METHOD

DRIP ☐ ESPRESSO ☐ PRESS ☐

POUR-OVER ☐ SIPHON ☐ OTHER ____________

NOTES ____________

RECOMMEND TO ____________

COFFEE NAME ______________________ DATE ____________

BEVERAGE ______________________

PLACE TASTED ______________________ PRICE ____________

COUNTRY / REGION ______________________

COMPANY ______________________

TESTING RATING

	0.5	1	1.5	2	2.5	3	3.5	4	4.5	5
APPEARANCE										
AROMA										
FLAVOR										

	0.5	1	1.5	2	2.5	3	3.5	4	4.5	5
SWEET										
ACIDIC										
SPICY										
CITRUS										
CHOCOLATE										
CARAMEL										
BITTER										
SAVORY										

BREW METHOD

DRIP ☐ ESPRESSO ☐ PRESS ☐

POUR-OVER ☐ SIPHON ☐ OTHER ________

NOTES ______________________

RECOMMEND TO ______________________

COFFEE NAME ______________________ DATE ____________

BEVERAGE ______________________

PLACE TASTED ______________________ PRICE ____________

COUNTRY / REGION ______________________

COMPANY ______________________

TESTING RATING

	0.5	1	1.5	2	2.5	3	3.5	4	4.5	5
APPEARANCE										
AROMA										
FLAVOR										

	0.5	1	1.5	2	2.5	3	3.5	4	4.5	5
SWEET										
ACIDIC										
SPICY										
CITRUS										
CHOCOLATE										
CARAMEL										
BITTER										
SAVORY										

BREW METHOD

DRIP ☐ ESPRESSO ☐ PRESS ☐

POUR-OVER ☐ SIPHON ☐ OTHER ________

NOTES

RECOMMEND TO

COFFEE NAME ______________________ DATE ____________

BEVERAGE ______________________

PLACE TASTED ______________________ PRICE ____________

COUNTRY / REGION ______________________

COMPANY ______________________

TESTING RATING

	0.5	1	1.5	2	2.5	3	3.5	4	4.5	5
APPEARANCE										
AROMA										
FLAVOR										

	0.5	1	1.5	2	2.5	3	3.5	4	4.5	5
SWEET										
ACIDIC										
SPICY										
CITRUS										
CHOCOLATE										
CARAMEL										
BITTER										
SAVORY										

BREW METHOD

DRIP ☐ ESPRESSO ☐ PRESS ☐

POUR-OVER ☐ SIPHON ☐ OTHER ________

NOTES ______________________

RECOMMEND TO ______________________

COFFEE NAME ______________________ DATE ____________

BEVERAGE ______________________

PLACE TASTED ______________________ PRICE ____________

COUNTRY / REGION ______________________

COMPANY ______________________

TESTING RATING

	0.5	1	1.5	2	2.5	3	3.5	4	4.5	5
APPEARANCE										
AROMA										
FLAVOR										

	0.5	1	1.5	2	2.5	3	3.5	4	4.5	5
SWEET										
ACIDIC										
SPICY										
CITRUS										
CHOCOLATE										
CARAMEL										
BITTER										
SAVORY										

BREW METHOD

DRIP ☐ ESPRESSO ☐ PRESS ☐

POUR-OVER ☐ SIPHON ☐ OTHER ________

NOTES ______________________

RECOMMEND TO ______________________

COFFEE NAME ____________________ DATE __________

BEVERAGE ____________________

PLACE TASTED ____________________ PRICE __________

COUNTRY / REGION ____________________

COMPANY ____________________

TESTING RATING

	0.5	1	1.5	2	2.5	3	3.5	4	4.5	5
APPEARANCE										
AROMA										
FLAVOR										

	0.5	1	1.5	2	2.5	3	3.5	4	4.5	5
SWEET										
ACIDIC										
SPICY										
CITRUS										
CHOCOLATE										
CARAMEL										
BITTER										
SAVORY										

BREW METHOD

DRIP ☐ ESPRESSO ☐ PRESS ☐

POUR-OVER ☐ SIPHON ☐ OTHER __________

NOTES ____________________

RECOMMEND TO ____________________

COFFEE NAME ______________________ DATE ____________

BEVERAGE ______________________

PLACE TASTED ______________________ PRICE ____________

COUNTRY / REGION ______________________

COMPANY ______________________

TESTING RATING

	0.5	1	1.5	2	2.5	3	3.5	4	4.5	5
APPEARANCE										
AROMA										
FLAVOR										

	0.5	1	1.5	2	2.5	3	3.5	4	4.5	5
SWEET										
ACIDIC										
SPICY										
CITRUS										
CHOCOLATE										
CARAMEL										
BITTER										
SAVORY										

BREW METHOD

DRIP ☐ ESPRESSO ☐ PRESS ☐

POUR-OVER ☐ SIPHON ☐ OTHER ________

NOTES ______________________

RECOMMEND TO ______________________

COFFEE NAME ______________________ DATE ____________

BEVERAGE ______________________

PLACE TASTED ______________________ PRICE ____________

COUNTRY / REGION ______________________

COMPANY ______________________

TESTING RATING

	0.5	1	1.5	2	2.5	3	3.5	4	4.5	5
APPEARANCE										
AROMA										
FLAVOR										

	0.5	1	1.5	2	2.5	3	3.5	4	4.5	5
SWEET										
ACIDIC										
SPICY										
CITRUS										
CHOCOLATE										
CARAMEL										
BITTER										
SAVORY										

BREW METHOD

DRIP ☐ ESPRESSO ☐ PRESS ☐

POUR-OVER ☐ SIPHON ☐ OTHER ________

NOTES ______________________

RECOMMEND TO ______________________

COFFEE NAME ______________________ DATE ____________

BEVERAGE ______________________

PLACE TASTED ______________________ PRICE ____________

COUNTRY / REGION ______________________

COMPANY ______________________

TESTING RATING

	0.5	1	1.5	2	2.5	3	3.5	4	4.5	5
APPEARANCE										
AROMA										
FLAVOR										

	0.5	1	1.5	2	2.5	3	3.5	4	4.5	5
SWEET										
ACIDIC										
SPICY										
CITRUS										
CHOCOLATE										
CARAMEL										
BITTER										
SAVORY										

BREW METHOD

DRIP ☐ ESPRESSO ☐ PRESS ☐

POUR-OVER ☐ SIPHON ☐ OTHER ________

NOTES

____

RECOMMEND TO

____

COFFEE NAME ______________________ DATE ____________

BEVERAGE ______________________

PLACE TASTED ______________________ PRICE ____________

COUNTRY / REGION ______________________

COMPANY ______________________

TESTING RATING

	0.5	1	1.5	2	2.5	3	3.5	4	4.5	5
APPEARANCE										
AROMA										
FLAVOR										

	0.5	1	1.5	2	2.5	3	3.5	4	4.5	5
SWEET										
ACIDIC										
SPICY										
CITRUS										
CHOCOLATE										
CARAMEL										
BITTER										
SAVORY										

BREW METHOD

DRIP ☐ ESPRESSO ☐ PRESS ☐

POUR-OVER ☐ SIPHON ☐ OTHER ________

NOTES ______________________

RECOMMEND TO ______________________

COFFEE NAME ______________________ DATE ____________

BEVERAGE ______________________

PLACE TASTED ______________________ PRICE ____________

COUNTRY / REGION ______________________

COMPANY ______________________

TESTING RATING

	0.5	1	1.5	2	2.5	3	3.5	4	4.5	5
APPEARANCE										
AROMA										
FLAVOR										

	0.5	1	1.5	2	2.5	3	3.5	4	4.5	5
SWEET										
ACIDIC										
SPICY										
CITRUS										
CHOCOLATE										
CARAMEL										
BITTER										
SAVORY										

BREW METHOD

DRIP ☐ ESPRESSO ☐ PRESS ☐

POUR-OVER ☐ SIPHON ☐ OTHER ____________

NOTES ______________________

RECOMMEND TO ______________________

COFFEE NAME ______________________ DATE ____________

BEVERAGE ______________________

PLACE TASTED ______________________ PRICE ____________

COUNTRY / REGION ______________________

COMPANY ______________________

TESTING RATING

	0.5	1	1.5	2	2.5	3	3.5	4	4.5	5
APPEARANCE										
AROMA										
FLAVOR										

	0.5	1	1.5	2	2.5	3	3.5	4	4.5	5
SWEET										
ACIDIC										
SPICY										
CITRUS										
CHOCOLATE										
CARAMEL										
BITTER										
SAVORY										

BREW METHOD

DRIP ☐ ESPRESSO ☐ PRESS ☐

POUR-OVER ☐ SIPHON ☐ OTHER ________

NOTES ______________________

RECOMMEND TO ______________________

COFFEE NAME ______________________ DATE ____________

BEVERAGE ______________________

PLACE TASTED ______________________ PRICE ____________

COUNTRY / REGION ______________________

COMPANY ______________________

TESTING RATING

	0.5	1	1.5	2	2.5	3	3.5	4	4.5	5
APPEARANCE										
AROMA										
FLAVOR										

	0.5	1	1.5	2	2.5	3	3.5	4	4.5	5
SWEET										
ACIDIC										
SPICY										
CITRUS										
CHOCOLATE										
CARAMEL										
BITTER										
SAVORY										

BREW METHOD

DRIP ☐ ESPRESSO ☐ PRESS ☐

POUR-OVER ☐ SIPHON ☐ OTHER ________

NOTES ______________________

RECOMMEND TO ______________________

COFFEE NAME ______________________ DATE ____________

BEVERAGE ______________________

PLACE TASTED ______________________ PRICE ____________

COUNTRY / REGION ______________________

COMPANY ______________________

TESTING RATING

	0.5	1	1.5	2	2.5	3	3.5	4	4.5	5
APPEARANCE										
AROMA										
FLAVOR										

	0.5	1	1.5	2	2.5	3	3.5	4	4.5	5
SWEET										
ACIDIC										
SPICY										
CITRUS										
CHOCOLATE										
CARAMEL										
BITTER										
SAVORY										

BREW METHOD

DRIP ☐ ESPRESSO ☐ PRESS ☐

POUR-OVER ☐ SIPHON ☐ OTHER ________

NOTES ______________________

RECOMMEND TO ______________________

COFFEE NAME ______________________ DATE ____________

BEVERAGE ______________________

PLACE TASTED ______________________ PRICE ____________

COUNTRY / REGION ______________________

COMPANY ______________________

TESTING RATING

	0.5	1	1.5	2	2.5	3	3.5	4	4.5	5
APPEARANCE										
AROMA										
FLAVOR										

	0.5	1	1.5	2	2.5	3	3.5	4	4.5	5
SWEET										
ACIDIC										
SPICY										
CITRUS										
CHOCOLATE										
CARAMEL										
BITTER										
SAVORY										

BREW METHOD

DRIP ☐ ESPRESSO ☐ PRESS ☐

POUR-OVER ☐ SIPHON ☐ OTHER ________

NOTES ______________________

RECOMMEND TO ______________________

COFFEE NAME ______________________ DATE ____________

BEVERAGE ______________________

PLACE TASTED ______________________ PRICE ____________

COUNTRY / REGION ______________________

COMPANY ______________________

TESTING RATING

	0.5	1	1.5	2	2.5	3	3.5	4	4.5	5
APPEARANCE										
AROMA										
FLAVOR										

	0.5	1	1.5	2	2.5	3	3.5	4	4.5	5
SWEET										
ACIDIC										
SPICY										
CITRUS										
CHOCOLATE										
CARAMEL										
BITTER										
SAVORY										

BREW METHOD

DRIP ☐ ESPRESSO ☐ PRESS ☐

POUR-OVER ☐ SIPHON ☐ OTHER ________

NOTES

____

RECOMMEND TO

____

COFFEE NAME ____________________ DATE ____________

BEVERAGE ____________________

PLACE TASTED ____________________ PRICE ____________

COUNTRY / REGION ____________________

COMPANY ____________________

TESTING RATING

	0.5	1	1.5	2	2.5	3	3.5	4	4.5	5
APPEARANCE										
AROMA										
FLAVOR										

	0.5	1	1.5	2	2.5	3	3.5	4	4.5	5
SWEET										
ACIDIC										
SPICY										
CITRUS										
CHOCOLATE										
CARAMEL										
BITTER										
SAVORY										

BREW METHOD

DRIP ☐ ESPRESSO ☐ PRESS ☐

POUR-OVER ☐ SIPHON ☐ OTHER ____________

NOTES ____________________

RECOMMEND TO ____________________

COFFEE NAME ______________________ DATE ____________

BEVERAGE ______________________

PLACE TASTED ______________________ PRICE ____________

COUNTRY / REGION ______________________

COMPANY ______________________

TESTING RATING

	0.5	1	1.5	2	2.5	3	3.5	4	4.5	5
APPEARANCE										
AROMA										
FLAVOR										

	0.5	1	1.5	2	2.5	3	3.5	4	4.5	5
SWEET										
ACIDIC										
SPICY										
CITRUS										
CHOCOLATE										
CARAMEL										
BITTER										
SAVORY										

BREW METHOD

DRIP ☐ ESPRESSO ☐ PRESS ☐

POUR-OVER ☐ SIPHON ☐ OTHER ________

NOTES ______________________

RECOMMEND TO ______________________

COFFEE NAME ____________________ DATE ____________

BEVERAGE ____________________

PLACE TASTED ____________________ PRICE ____________

COUNTRY / REGION ____________________

COMPANY ____________________

TESTING RATING

	0.5	1	1.5	2	2.5	3	3.5	4	4.5	5
APPEARANCE										
AROMA										
FLAVOR										

	0.5	1	1.5	2	2.5	3	3.5	4	4.5	5
SWEET										
ACIDIC										
SPICY										
CITRUS										
CHOCOLATE										
CARAMEL										
BITTER										
SAVORY										

BREW METHOD

DRIP ☐ ESPRESSO ☐ PRESS ☐

POUR-OVER ☐ SIPHON ☐ OTHER ________

NOTES

RECOMMEND TO

COFFEE NAME ______________________ DATE ____________

BEVERAGE ______________________

PLACE TASTED ______________________ PRICE ____________

COUNTRY / REGION ______________________

COMPANY ______________________

TESTING RATING

	0.5	1	1.5	2	2.5	3	3.5	4	4.5	5
APPEARANCE										
AROMA										
FLAVOR										

BREW METHOD

DRIP ☐ ESPRESSO ☐ PRESS ☐

POUR-OVER ☐ SIPHON ☐ OTHER ________

	0.5	1	1.5	2	2.5	3	3.5	4	4.5	5
SWEET										
ACIDIC										
SPICY										
CITRUS										
CHOCOLATE										
CARAMEL										
BITTER										
SAVORY										

NOTES ______________________

RECOMMEND TO ______________________

COFFEE NAME ______________________ DATE ____________

BEVERAGE ______________________

PLACE TASTED ______________________ PRICE ____________

COUNTRY / REGION ______________________

COMPANY ______________________

TESTING RATING

	0.5	1	1.5	2	2.5	3	3.5	4	4.5	5
APPEARANCE										
AROMA										
FLAVOR										

	0.5	1	1.5	2	2.5	3	3.5	4	4.5	5
SWEET										
ACIDIC										
SPICY										
CITRUS										
CHOCOLATE										
CARAMEL										
BITTER										
SAVORY										

BREW METHOD

DRIP ☐ ESPRESSO ☐ PRESS ☐

POUR-OVER ☐ SIPHON ☐ OTHER ________

NOTES ______________________

RECOMMEND TO ______________________

COFFEE NAME ______________________ DATE ____________

BEVERAGE ______________________

PLACE TASTED ______________________ PRICE ____________

COUNTRY / REGION ______________________

COMPANY ______________________

TESTING RATING

	0.5	1	1.5	2	2.5	3	3.5	4	4.5	5
APPEARANCE										
AROMA										
FLAVOR										

	0.5	1	1.5	2	2.5	3	3.5	4	4.5	5
SWEET										
ACIDIC										
SPICY										
CITRUS										
CHOCOLATE										
CARAMEL										
BITTER										
SAVORY										

BREW METHOD

DRIP ☐ ESPRESSO ☐ PRESS ☐

POUR-OVER ☐ SIPHON ☐ OTHER ________

NOTES ______________________

RECOMMEND TO ______________________

COFFEE NAME ______________________ DATE ____________

BEVERAGE ______________________

PLACE TASTED ______________________ PRICE ____________

COUNTRY / REGION ______________________

COMPANY ______________________

TESTING RATING

	0.5	1	1.5	2	2.5	3	3.5	4	4.5	5
APPEARANCE										
AROMA										
FLAVOR										

	0.5	1	1.5	2	2.5	3	3.5	4	4.5	5
SWEET										
ACIDIC										
SPICY										
CITRUS										
CHOCOLATE										
CARAMEL										
BITTER										
SAVORY										

BREW METHOD

DRIP ☐ ESPRESSO ☐ PRESS ☐

POUR-OVER ☐ SIPHON ☐ OTHER ________

NOTES

____

RECOMMEND TO

____

COFFEE NAME ______________________ DATE ____________

BEVERAGE ______________________

PLACE TASTED ______________________ PRICE ____________

COUNTRY / REGION ______________________

COMPANY ______________________

TESTING RATING

	0.5	1	1.5	2	2.5	3	3.5	4	4.5	5
APPEARANCE										
AROMA										
FLAVOR										

	0.5	1	1.5	2	2.5	3	3.5	4	4.5	5
SWEET										
ACIDIC										
SPICY										
CITRUS										
CHOCOLATE										
CARAMEL										
BITTER										
SAVORY										

BREW METHOD

DRIP ☐ ESPRESSO ☐ PRESS ☐

POUR-OVER ☐ SIPHON ☐ OTHER ________

NOTES ______________________

RECOMMEND TO ______________________

COFFEE NAME ______________________ DATE ____________

BEVERAGE ______________________

PLACE TASTED ______________________ PRICE ____________

COUNTRY / REGION ______________________

COMPANY ______________________

TESTING RATING

	0.5	1	1.5	2	2.5	3	3.5	4	4.5	5
APPEARANCE										
AROMA										
FLAVOR										

	0.5	1	1.5	2	2.5	3	3.5	4	4.5	5
SWEET										
ACIDIC										
SPICY										
CITRUS										
CHOCOLATE										
CARAMEL										
BITTER										
SAVORY										

BREW METHOD

DRIP ☐ ESPRESSO ☐ PRESS ☐

POUR-OVER ☐ SIPHON ☐ OTHER ________

NOTES ______________________

RECOMMEND TO ______________________

COFFEE NAME ______________________ DATE ____________

BEVERAGE ______________________

PLACE TASTED ______________________ PRICE ____________

COUNTRY / REGION ______________________

COMPANY ______________________

TESTING RATING

	0.5	1	1.5	2	2.5	3	3.5	4	4.5	5
APPEARANCE										
AROMA										
FLAVOR										

	0.5	1	1.5	2	2.5	3	3.5	4	4.5	5
SWEET										
ACIDIC										
SPICY										
CITRUS										
CHOCOLATE										
CARAMEL										
BITTER										
SAVORY										

BREW METHOD

DRIP ☐ ESPRESSO ☐ PRESS ☐

POUR-OVER ☐ SIPHON ☐ OTHER ________

NOTES ______________________

RECOMMEND TO ______________________

COFFEE NAME ______________________ DATE ____________

BEVERAGE ______________________

PLACE TASTED ______________________ PRICE ____________

COUNTRY / REGION ______________________

COMPANY ______________________

TESTING RATING

	0.5	1	1.5	2	2.5	3	3.5	4	4.5	5
APPEARANCE										
AROMA										
FLAVOR										

	0.5	1	1.5	2	2.5	3	3.5	4	4.5	5
SWEET										
ACIDIC										
SPICY										
CITRUS										
CHOCOLATE										
CARAMEL										
BITTER										
SAVORY										

BREW METHOD

DRIP ☐ ESPRESSO ☐ PRESS ☐

POUR-OVER ☐ SIPHON ☐ OTHER ________

NOTES ______________________

RECOMMEND TO ______________________

COFFEE NAME ______________________ DATE ____________

BEVERAGE ______________________

PLACE TASTED ______________________ PRICE ____________

COUNTRY / REGION ______________________

COMPANY ______________________

TESTING RATING

	0.5	1	1.5	2	2.5	3	3.5	4	4.5	5
APPEARANCE										
AROMA										
FLAVOR										

	0.5	1	1.5	2	2.5	3	3.5	4	4.5	5
SWEET										
ACIDIC										
SPICY										
CITRUS										
CHOCOLATE										
CARAMEL										
BITTER										
SAVORY										

BREW METHOD

DRIP ☐ ESPRESSO ☐ PRESS ☐

POUR-OVER ☐ SIPHON ☐ OTHER ________

NOTES ______________________

RECOMMEND TO ______________________

COFFEE NAME ____________________ DATE ____________

BEVERAGE ____________________

PLACE TASTED ____________________ PRICE ____________

COUNTRY / REGION ____________________

COMPANY ____________________

TESTING RATING

	0.5	1	1.5	2	2.5	3	3.5	4	4.5	5
APPEARANCE										
AROMA										
FLAVOR										

	0.5	1	1.5	2	2.5	3	3.5	4	4.5	5
SWEET										
ACIDIC										
SPICY										
CITRUS										
CHOCOLATE										
CARAMEL										
BITTER										
SAVORY										

BREW METHOD

DRIP ☐ ESPRESSO ☐ PRESS ☐

POUR-OVER ☐ SIPHON ☐ OTHER ________

NOTES ____________________

RECOMMEND TO ____________________

COFFEE NAME ____________ DATE ____________

BEVERAGE ____________

PLACE TASTED ____________ PRICE ____________

COUNTRY / REGION ____________

COMPANY ____________

TESTING RATING

	0.5	1	1.5	2	2.5	3	3.5	4	4.5	5
APPEARANCE										
AROMA										
FLAVOR										

	0.5	1	1.5	2	2.5	3	3.5	4	4.5	5
SWEET										
ACIDIC										
SPICY										
CITRUS										
CHOCOLATE										
CARAMEL										
BITTER										
SAVORY										

BREW METHOD

DRIP ☐ ESPRESSO ☐ PRESS ☐

POUR-OVER ☐ SIPHON ☐ OTHER ____________

NOTES ____________

RECOMMEND TO ____________

COFFEE NAME ____________________ DATE ____________

BEVERAGE ____________________

PLACE TASTED ____________________ PRICE ____________

COUNTRY / REGION ____________________

COMPANY ____________________

TESTING RATING

	0.5	1	1.5	2	2.5	3	3.5	4	4.5	5
APPEARANCE										
AROMA										
FLAVOR										

	0.5	1	1.5	2	2.5	3	3.5	4	4.5	5
SWEET										
ACIDIC										
SPICY										
CITRUS										
CHOCOLATE										
CARAMEL										
BITTER										
SAVORY										

BREW METHOD

DRIP ☐ ESPRESSO ☐ PRESS ☐

POUR-OVER ☐ SIPHON ☐ OTHER ________

NOTES ____________________

RECOMMEND TO ____________________

COFFEE NAME ______________________ DATE ____________

BEVERAGE ______________________

PLACE TASTED ______________________ PRICE ____________

COUNTRY / REGION ______________________

COMPANY ______________________

TESTING RATING

	0.5	1	1.5	2	2.5	3	3.5	4	4.5	5
APPEARANCE										
AROMA										
FLAVOR										

	0.5	1	1.5	2	2.5	3	3.5	4	4.5	5
SWEET										
ACIDIC										
SPICY										
CITRUS										
CHOCOLATE										
CARAMEL										
BITTER										
SAVORY										

BREW METHOD

DRIP ☐ ESPRESSO ☐ PRESS ☐

POUR-OVER ☐ SIPHON ☐ OTHER ________

NOTES ______________________

RECOMMEND TO ______________________

COFFEE NAME ______________________ DATE ____________

BEVERAGE ______________________

PLACE TASTED ______________________ PRICE ____________

COUNTRY / REGION ______________________

COMPANY ______________________

TESTING RATING

	0.5	1	1.5	2	2.5	3	3.5	4	4.5	5
APPEARANCE										
AROMA										
FLAVOR										

	0.5	1	1.5	2	2.5	3	3.5	4	4.5	5
SWEET										
ACIDIC										
SPICY										
CITRUS										
CHOCOLATE										
CARAMEL										
BITTER										
SAVORY										

BREW METHOD

DRIP ☐ ESPRESSO ☐ PRESS ☐

POUR-OVER ☐ SIPHON ☐ OTHER ______

NOTES

____

RECOMMEND TO

____

COFFEE NAME ______________________ DATE ____________

BEVERAGE ______________________

PLACE TASTED ______________________ PRICE ____________

COUNTRY / REGION ______________________

COMPANY ______________________

TESTING RATING

	0.5	1	1.5	2	2.5	3	3.5	4	4.5	5
APPEARANCE										
AROMA										
FLAVOR										

	0.5	1	1.5	2	2.5	3	3.5	4	4.5	5
SWEET										
ACIDIC										
SPICY										
CITRUS										
CHOCOLATE										
CARAMEL										
BITTER										
SAVORY										

BREW METHOD

DRIP ☐ ESPRESSO ☐ PRESS ☐

POUR-OVER ☐ SIPHON ☐ OTHER ________

NOTES

____

RECOMMEND TO

____

COFFEE NAME ____________________ DATE ____________

BEVERAGE ____________________

PLACE TASTED ____________________ PRICE ____________

COUNTRY / REGION ____________________

COMPANY ____________________

TESTING RATING

	0.5	1	1.5	2	2.5	3	3.5	4	4.5	5
APPEARANCE										
AROMA										
FLAVOR										

	0.5	1	1.5	2	2.5	3	3.5	4	4.5	5
SWEET										
ACIDIC										
SPICY										
CITRUS										
CHOCOLATE										
CARAMEL										
BITTER										
SAVORY										

BREW METHOD

DRIP ☐ ESPRESSO ☐ PRESS ☐

POUR-OVER ☐ SIPHON ☐ OTHER ________

NOTES ____________________

RECOMMEND TO ____________________

COFFEE NAME ______________________ DATE ____________

BEVERAGE ______________________

PLACE TASTED ______________________ PRICE ____________

COUNTRY / REGION ______________________

COMPANY ______________________

TESTING RATING

	0.5	1	1.5	2	2.5	3	3.5	4	4.5	5
APPEARANCE										
AROMA										
FLAVOR										

	0.5	1	1.5	2	2.5	3	3.5	4	4.5	5
SWEET										
ACIDIC										
SPICY										
CITRUS										
CHOCOLATE										
CARAMEL										
BITTER										
SAVORY										

BREW METHOD

DRIP ☐ ESPRESSO ☐ PRESS ☐

POUR-OVER ☐ SIPHON ☐ OTHER ________

NOTES ______________________

RECOMMEND TO ______________________

COFFEE NAME ____________________ DATE ____________

BEVERAGE ____________________

PLACE TASTED ____________________ PRICE ____________

COUNTRY / REGION ____________________

COMPANY ____________________

TESTING RATING

	0.5	1	1.5	2	2.5	3	3.5	4	4.5	5
APPEARANCE										
AROMA										
FLAVOR										

	0.5	1	1.5	2	2.5	3	3.5	4	4.5	5
SWEET										
ACIDIC										
SPICY										
CITRUS										
CHOCOLATE										
CARAMEL										
BITTER										
SAVORY										

BREW METHOD

DRIP ☐ ESPRESSO ☐ PRESS ☐

POUR-OVER ☐ SIPHON ☐ OTHER ________

NOTES

RECOMMEND TO

COFFEE NAME ____________________ DATE ____________

BEVERAGE ____________________

PLACE TASTED ____________________ PRICE ____________

COUNTRY / REGION ____________________

COMPANY ____________________

TESTING RATING

	0.5	1	1.5	2	2.5	3	3.5	4	4.5	5
APPEARANCE										
AROMA										
FLAVOR										

	0.5	1	1.5	2	2.5	3	3.5	4	4.5	5
SWEET										
ACIDIC										
SPICY										
CITRUS										
CHOCOLATE										
CARAMEL										
BITTER										
SAVORY										

BREW METHOD

DRIP ☐ ESPRESSO ☐ PRESS ☐

POUR-OVER ☐ SIPHON ☐ OTHER ________

NOTES ____________________

RECOMMEND TO ____________________

COFFEE NAME ______________________ DATE ____________

BEVERAGE ______________________

PLACE TASTED ______________________ PRICE ____________

COUNTRY / REGION ______________________

COMPANY ______________________

TESTING RATING

	0.5	1	1.5	2	2.5	3	3.5	4	4.5	5
APPEARANCE										
AROMA										
FLAVOR										

	0.5	1	1.5	2	2.5	3	3.5	4	4.5	5
SWEET										
ACIDIC										
SPICY										
CITRUS										
CHOCOLATE										
CARAMEL										
BITTER										
SAVORY										

BREW METHOD

DRIP ☐ ESPRESSO ☐ PRESS ☐

POUR-OVER ☐ SIPHON ☐ OTHER ________

NOTES ______________________

RECOMMEND TO ______________________

COFFEE NAME ____________________ DATE ____________

BEVERAGE ____________________

PLACE TASTED ____________________ PRICE ____________

COUNTRY / REGION ____________________

COMPANY ____________________

TESTING RATING

	0.5	1	1.5	2	2.5	3	3.5	4	4.5	5
APPEARANCE										
AROMA										
FLAVOR										

	0.5	1	1.5	2	2.5	3	3.5	4	4.5	5
SWEET										
ACIDIC										
SPICY										
CITRUS										
CHOCOLATE										
CARAMEL										
BITTER										
SAVORY										

BREW METHOD

DRIP ☐ ESPRESSO ☐ PRESS ☐

POUR-OVER ☐ SIPHON ☐ OTHER ________

NOTES ____________________

RECOMMEND TO ____________________

COFFEE NAME ____________________ DATE ____________

BEVERAGE ____________________

PLACE TASTED ____________________ PRICE ____________

COUNTRY / REGION ____________________

COMPANY ____________________

TESTING RATING

	0.5	1	1.5	2	2.5	3	3.5	4	4.5	5
APPEARANCE										
AROMA										
FLAVOR										

	0.5	1	1.5	2	2.5	3	3.5	4	4.5	5
SWEET										
ACIDIC										
SPICY										
CITRUS										
CHOCOLATE										
CARAMEL										
BITTER										
SAVORY										

BREW METHOD

DRIP ☐ ESPRESSO ☐ PRESS ☐

POUR-OVER ☐ SIPHON ☐ OTHER ________

NOTES

RECOMMEND TO

COFFEE NAME ______________________ DATE ____________

BEVERAGE ______________________

PLACE TASTED ______________________ PRICE ____________

COUNTRY / REGION ______________________

COMPANY ______________________

TESTING RATING

	0.5	1	1.5	2	2.5	3	3.5	4	4.5	5
APPEARANCE										
AROMA										
FLAVOR										

	0.5	1	1.5	2	2.5	3	3.5	4	4.5	5
SWEET										
ACIDIC										
SPICY										
CITRUS										
CHOCOLATE										
CARAMEL										
BITTER										
SAVORY										

BREW METHOD

DRIP ☐ ESPRESSO ☐ PRESS ☐

POUR-OVER ☐ SIPHON ☐ OTHER ________

NOTES ______________________

RECOMMEND TO ______________________

COFFEE NAME ______________________ DATE ____________

BEVERAGE ______________________

PLACE TASTED ______________________ PRICE ____________

COUNTRY / REGION ______________________

COMPANY ______________________

TESTING RATING

	0.5	1	1.5	2	2.5	3	3.5	4	4.5	5
APPEARANCE										
AROMA										
FLAVOR										

	0.5	1	1.5	2	2.5	3	3.5	4	4.5	5
SWEET										
ACIDIC										
SPICY										
CITRUS										
CHOCOLATE										
CARAMEL										
BITTER										
SAVORY										

BREW METHOD

DRIP ☐ ESPRESSO ☐ PRESS ☐

POUR-OVER ☐ SIPHON ☐ OTHER ________

NOTES ______________________

RECOMMEND TO ______________________

COFFEE NAME ______________________ DATE ____________

BEVERAGE ______________________

PLACE TASTED ______________________ PRICE ____________

COUNTRY / REGION ______________________

COMPANY ______________________

TESTING RATING

	0.5	1	1.5	2	2.5	3	3.5	4	4.5	5
APPEARANCE										
AROMA										
FLAVOR										

	0.5	1	1.5	2	2.5	3	3.5	4	4.5	5
SWEET										
ACIDIC										
SPICY										
CITRUS										
CHOCOLATE										
CARAMEL										
BITTER										
SAVORY										

BREW METHOD

DRIP ☐ ESPRESSO ☐ PRESS ☐

POUR-OVER ☐ SIPHON ☐ OTHER ________

NOTES

RECOMMEND TO

COFFEE NAME ______________________ DATE ____________

BEVERAGE ______________________

PLACE TASTED ______________________ PRICE ____________

COUNTRY / REGION ______________________

COMPANY ______________________

TESTING RATING

	0.5	1	1.5	2	2.5	3	3.5	4	4.5	5
APPEARANCE										
AROMA										
FLAVOR										

	0.5	1	1.5	2	2.5	3	3.5	4	4.5	5
SWEET										
ACIDIC										
SPICY										
CITRUS										
CHOCOLATE										
CARAMEL										
BITTER										
SAVORY										

BREW METHOD

DRIP ☐ ESPRESSO ☐ PRESS ☐

POUR-OVER ☐ SIPHON ☐ OTHER ________

NOTES ______________________

RECOMMEND TO ______________________

COFFEE NAME ____________________ DATE __________

BEVERAGE ____________________

PLACE TASTED ____________________ PRICE __________

COUNTRY / REGION ____________________

COMPANY ____________________

TESTING RATING

	0.5	1	1.5	2	2.5	3	3.5	4	4.5	5
APPEARANCE										
AROMA										
FLAVOR										

	0.5	1	1.5	2	2.5	3	3.5	4	4.5	5
SWEET										
ACIDIC										
SPICY										
CITRUS										
CHOCOLATE										
CARAMEL										
BITTER										
SAVORY										

BREW METHOD

DRIP ☐ ESPRESSO ☐ PRESS ☐

POUR-OVER ☐ SIPHON ☐ OTHER __________

NOTES ____________________

RECOMMEND TO ____________________

COFFEE NAME ____________________ DATE ____________

BEVERAGE ____________________

PLACE TASTED ____________________ PRICE ____________

COUNTRY / REGION ____________________

COMPANY ____________________

TESTING RATING

	0.5	1	1.5	2	2.5	3	3.5	4	4.5	5
APPEARANCE										
AROMA										
FLAVOR										

	0.5	1	1.5	2	2.5	3	3.5	4	4.5	5
SWEET										
ACIDIC										
SPICY										
CITRUS										
CHOCOLATE										
CARAMEL										
BITTER										
SAVORY										

BREW METHOD

DRIP ☐ ESPRESSO ☐ PRESS ☐

POUR-OVER ☐ SIPHON ☐ OTHER ________

NOTES ____________________

RECOMMEND TO ____________________

COFFEE NAME ______________________ DATE ____________

BEVERAGE ______________________

PLACE TASTED ______________________ PRICE ____________

COUNTRY / REGION ______________________

COMPANY ______________________

TESTING RATING

	0.5	1	1.5	2	2.5	3	3.5	4	4.5	5
APPEARANCE										
AROMA										
FLAVOR										

	0.5	1	1.5	2	2.5	3	3.5	4	4.5	5
SWEET										
ACIDIC										
SPICY										
CITRUS										
CHOCOLATE										
CARAMEL										
BITTER										
SAVORY										

BREW METHOD

DRIP ☐ ESPRESSO ☐ PRESS ☐

POUR-OVER ☐ SIPHON ☐ OTHER ________

NOTES ______________________

RECOMMEND TO ______________________

COFFEE NAME ______________________ DATE ____________

BEVERAGE ______________________

PLACE TASTED ______________________ PRICE ____________

COUNTRY / REGION ______________________

COMPANY ______________________

TESTING RATING

	0.5	1	1.5	2	2.5	3	3.5	4	4.5	5
APPEARANCE										
AROMA										
FLAVOR										

	0.5	1	1.5	2	2.5	3	3.5	4	4.5	5
SWEET										
ACIDIC										
SPICY										
CITRUS										
CHOCOLATE										
CARAMEL										
BITTER										
SAVORY										

BREW METHOD

DRIP ☐ ESPRESSO ☐ PRESS ☐

POUR-OVER ☐ SIPHON ☐ OTHER ________

NOTES

RECOMMEND TO

COFFEE NAME ______________________ DATE ____________

BEVERAGE ______________________

PLACE TASTED ______________________ PRICE ____________

COUNTRY / REGION ______________________

COMPANY ______________________

TESTING RATING

	0.5	1	1.5	2	2.5	3	3.5	4	4.5	5
APPEARANCE										
AROMA										
FLAVOR										

	0.5	1	1.5	2	2.5	3	3.5	4	4.5	5
SWEET										
ACIDIC										
SPICY										
CITRUS										
CHOCOLATE										
CARAMEL										
BITTER										
SAVORY										

BREW METHOD

DRIP ☐ ESPRESSO ☐ PRESS ☐

POUR-OVER ☐ SIPHON ☐ OTHER ________

NOTES ______________________

RECOMMEND TO ______________________

COFFEE NAME ______________________ DATE ____________

BEVERAGE ______________________

PLACE TASTED ______________________ PRICE ____________

COUNTRY / REGION ______________________

COMPANY ______________________

TESTING RATING

	0.5	1	1.5	2	2.5	3	3.5	4	4.5	5
APPEARANCE										
AROMA										
FLAVOR										

	0.5	1	1.5	2	2.5	3	3.5	4	4.5	5
SWEET										
ACIDIC										
SPICY										
CITRUS										
CHOCOLATE										
CARAMEL										
BITTER										
SAVORY										

BREW METHOD

DRIP ☐ ESPRESSO ☐ PRESS ☐

POUR-OVER ☐ SIPHON ☐ OTHER ________

NOTES ______________________

RECOMMEND TO ______________________

COFFEE NAME ______________________ DATE ______________

BEVERAGE ______________________

PLACE TASTED ______________________ PRICE ______________

COUNTRY / REGION ______________________

COMPANY ______________________

TESTING RATING

	0.5	1	1.5	2	2.5	3	3.5	4	4.5	5
APPEARANCE										
AROMA										
FLAVOR										

	0.5	1	1.5	2	2.5	3	3.5	4	4.5	5
SWEET										
ACIDIC										
SPICY										
CITRUS										
CHOCOLATE										
CARAMEL										
BITTER										
SAVORY										

BREW METHOD

DRIP ☐ ESPRESSO ☐ PRESS ☐

POUR-OVER ☐ SIPHON ☐ OTHER ______

NOTES ______________________

RECOMMEND TO ______________________

COFFEE NAME ______________________ DATE ____________

BEVERAGE ______________________

PLACE TASTED ______________________ PRICE ____________

COUNTRY / REGION ______________________

COMPANY ______________________

TESTING RATING

	0.5	1	1.5	2	2.5	3	3.5	4	4.5	5
APPEARANCE										
AROMA										
FLAVOR										

	0.5	1	1.5	2	2.5	3	3.5	4	4.5	5
SWEET										
ACIDIC										
SPICY										
CITRUS										
CHOCOLATE										
CARAMEL										
BITTER										
SAVORY										

BREW METHOD

DRIP ☐ ESPRESSO ☐ PRESS ☐

POUR-OVER ☐ SIPHON ☐ OTHER ______

NOTES ______________________

RECOMMEND TO ______________________

COFFEE NAME ______________________ DATE ______________

BEVERAGE ______________________

PLACE TASTED ______________________ PRICE ______________

COUNTRY / REGION ______________________

COMPANY ______________________

TESTING RATING

	0.5	1	1.5	2	2.5	3	3.5	4	4.5	5
APPEARANCE										
AROMA										
FLAVOR										

	0.5	1	1.5	2	2.5	3	3.5	4	4.5	5
SWEET										
ACIDIC										
SPICY										
CITRUS										
CHOCOLATE										
CARAMEL										
BITTER										
SAVORY										

BREW METHOD

DRIP ☐ ESPRESSO ☐ PRESS ☐

POUR-OVER ☐ SIPHON ☐ OTHER ______

NOTES ______________________

RECOMMEND TO ______________________

COFFEE NAME ____________________ DATE ____________

BEVERAGE ____________________

PLACE TASTED ____________________ PRICE ____________

COUNTRY / REGION ____________________

COMPANY ____________________

TESTING RATING

	0.5	1	1.5	2	2.5	3	3.5	4	4.5	5
APPEARANCE	☐	☐	☐	☐	☐	☐	☐	☐	☐	☐
AROMA	☐	☐	☐	☐	☐	☐	☐	☐	☐	☐
FLAVOR	☐	☐	☐	☐	☐	☐	☐	☐	☐	☐

BREW METHOD

DRIP ☐ ESPRESSO ☐ PRESS ☐

POUR-OVER ☐ SIPHON ☐ OTHER ________

	0.5	1	1.5	2	2.5	3	3.5	4	4.5	5
SWEET	☐	☐	☐	☐	☐	☐	☐	☐	☐	☐
ACIDIC	☐	☐	☐	☐	☐	☐	☐	☐	☐	☐
SPICY	☐	☐	☐	☐	☐	☐	☐	☐	☐	☐
CITRUS	☐	☐	☐	☐	☐	☐	☐	☐	☐	☐
CHOCOLATE	☐	☐	☐	☐	☐	☐	☐	☐	☐	☐
CARAMEL	☐	☐	☐	☐	☐	☐	☐	☐	☐	☐
BITTER	☐	☐	☐	☐	☐	☐	☐	☐	☐	☐
SAVORY	☐	☐	☐	☐	☐	☐	☐	☐	☐	☐

NOTES ____________________

RECOMMEND TO ____________________

COFFEE NAME ______________________ DATE ____________

BEVERAGE ______________________

PLACE TASTED ______________________ PRICE ____________

COUNTRY / REGION ______________________

COMPANY ______________________

TESTING RATING

	0.5	1	1.5	2	2.5	3	3.5	4	4.5	5
APPEARANCE										
AROMA										
FLAVOR										

	0.5	1	1.5	2	2.5	3	3.5	4	4.5	5
SWEET										
ACIDIC										
SPICY										
CITRUS										
CHOCOLATE										
CARAMEL										
BITTER										
SAVORY										

BREW METHOD

DRIP ☐ ESPRESSO ☐ PRESS ☐

POUR-OVER ☐ SIPHON ☐ OTHER ________

NOTES ______________________

RECOMMEND TO ______________________

COFFEE NAME ______________________ DATE ____________

BEVERAGE ______________________

PLACE TASTED ______________________ PRICE ____________

COUNTRY / REGION ______________________

COMPANY ______________________

TESTING RATING

	0.5	1	1.5	2	2.5	3	3.5	4	4.5	5
APPEARANCE										
AROMA										
FLAVOR										

	0.5	1	1.5	2	2.5	3	3.5	4	4.5	5
SWEET										
ACIDIC										
SPICY										
CITRUS										
CHOCOLATE										
CARAMEL										
BITTER										
SAVORY										

BREW METHOD

DRIP ☐ ESPRESSO ☐ PRESS ☐

POUR-OVER ☐ SIPHON ☐ OTHER ________

NOTES ______________________

RECOMMEND TO ______________________

COFFEE NAME ____________________ DATE ____________

BEVERAGE ____________________

PLACE TASTED ____________________ PRICE ____________

COUNTRY / REGION ____________________

COMPANY ____________________

TESTING RATING

	0.5	1	1.5	2	2.5	3	3.5	4	4.5	5
APPEARANCE										
AROMA										
FLAVOR										

	0.5	1	1.5	2	2.5	3	3.5	4	4.5	5
SWEET										
ACIDIC										
SPICY										
CITRUS										
CHOCOLATE										
CARAMEL										
BITTER										
SAVORY										

BREW METHOD

DRIP ☐ ESPRESSO ☐ PRESS ☐

POUR-OVER ☐ SIPHON ☐ OTHER ________

NOTES ____________________

RECOMMEND TO ____________________

COFFEE NAME ______________________ DATE ____________

BEVERAGE ______________________

PLACE TASTED ______________________ PRICE ____________

COUNTRY / REGION ______________________

COMPANY ______________________

TESTING RATING

	0.5	1	1.5	2	2.5	3	3.5	4	4.5	5
APPEARANCE										
AROMA										
FLAVOR										

	0.5	1	1.5	2	2.5	3	3.5	4	4.5	5
SWEET										
ACIDIC										
SPICY										
CITRUS										
CHOCOLATE										
CARAMEL										
BITTER										
SAVORY										

BREW METHOD

DRIP ☐ ESPRESSO ☐ PRESS ☐

POUR-OVER ☐ SIPHON ☐ OTHER ________

NOTES

RECOMMEND TO

COFFEE NAME ______________________ DATE ____________

BEVERAGE ______________________

PLACE TASTED ______________________ PRICE ____________

COUNTRY / REGION ______________________

COMPANY ______________________

TESTING RATING

	0.5	1	1.5	2	2.5	3	3.5	4	4.5	5
APPEARANCE										
AROMA										
FLAVOR										

	0.5	1	1.5	2	2.5	3	3.5	4	4.5	5
SWEET										
ACIDIC										
SPICY										
CITRUS										
CHOCOLATE										
CARAMEL										
BITTER										
SAVORY										

BREW METHOD

DRIP ☐ ESPRESSO ☐ PRESS ☐

POUR-OVER ☐ SIPHON ☐ OTHER ________

NOTES ______________________

RECOMMEND TO ______________________

COFFEE NAME ____________________ DATE __________

BEVERAGE ____________________

PLACE TASTED ____________________ PRICE __________

COUNTRY / REGION ____________________

COMPANY ____________________

TESTING RATING

	0.5	1	1.5	2	2.5	3	3.5	4	4.5	5
APPEARANCE										
AROMA										
FLAVOR										

	0.5	1	1.5	2	2.5	3	3.5	4	4.5	5
SWEET										
ACIDIC										
SPICY										
CITRUS										
CHOCOLATE										
CARAMEL										
BITTER										
SAVORY										

BREW METHOD

DRIP ☐ ESPRESSO ☐ PRESS ☐

POUR-OVER ☐ SIPHON ☐ OTHER ______

NOTES ____________________

RECOMMEND TO ____________________

COFFEE NAME ______________________ DATE ____________

BEVERAGE ______________________

PLACE TASTED ______________________ PRICE ____________

COUNTRY / REGION ______________________

COMPANY ______________________

TESTING RATING

	0.5	1	1.5	2	2.5	3	3.5	4	4.5	5
APPEARANCE										
AROMA										
FLAVOR										

	0.5	1	1.5	2	2.5	3	3.5	4	4.5	5
SWEET										
ACIDIC										
SPICY										
CITRUS										
CHOCOLATE										
CARAMEL										
BITTER										
SAVORY										

BREW METHOD

DRIP ☐ ESPRESSO ☐ PRESS ☐

POUR-OVER ☐ SIPHON ☐ OTHER ________

NOTES

RECOMMEND TO

COFFEE NAME ______________________ DATE ____________

BEVERAGE ______________________

PLACE TASTED ______________________ PRICE ____________

COUNTRY / REGION ______________________

COMPANY ______________________

TESTING RATING

	0.5	1	1.5	2	2.5	3	3.5	4	4.5	5
APPEARANCE										
AROMA										
FLAVOR										

	0.5	1	1.5	2	2.5	3	3.5	4	4.5	5
SWEET										
ACIDIC										
SPICY										
CITRUS										
CHOCOLATE										
CARAMEL										
BITTER										
SAVORY										

BREW METHOD

DRIP ☐ ESPRESSO ☐ PRESS ☐

POUR-OVER ☐ SIPHON ☐ OTHER ________

NOTES ______________________

RECOMMEND TO ______________________

COFFEE NAME ______________________ DATE ____________

BEVERAGE ______________________

PLACE TASTED ______________________ PRICE ____________

COUNTRY / REGION ______________________

COMPANY ______________________

TESTING RATING

	0.5	1	1.5	2	2.5	3	3.5	4	4.5	5
APPEARANCE										
AROMA										
FLAVOR										

	0.5	1	1.5	2	2.5	3	3.5	4	4.5	5
SWEET										
ACIDIC										
SPICY										
CITRUS										
CHOCOLATE										
CARAMEL										
BITTER										
SAVORY										

BREW METHOD

DRIP ☐ ESPRESSO ☐ PRESS ☐

POUR-OVER ☐ SIPHON ☐ OTHER ________

NOTES

RECOMMEND TO

COFFEE NAME ______________________ DATE ____________

BEVERAGE ______________________

PLACE TASTED ______________________ PRICE ____________

COUNTRY / REGION ______________________

COMPANY ______________________

TESTING RATING

	0.5	1	1.5	2	2.5	3	3.5	4	4.5	5
APPEARANCE										
AROMA										
FLAVOR										

	0.5	1	1.5	2	2.5	3	3.5	4	4.5	5
SWEET										
ACIDIC										
SPICY										
CITRUS										
CHOCOLATE										
CARAMEL										
BITTER										
SAVORY										

BREW METHOD

DRIP ☐ ESPRESSO ☐ PRESS ☐

POUR-OVER ☐ SIPHON ☐ OTHER ________

NOTES ______________________

RECOMMEND TO ______________________

COFFEE NAME ______________________ DATE ____________

BEVERAGE ______________________

PLACE TASTED ______________________ PRICE ____________

COUNTRY / REGION ______________________

COMPANY ______________________

TESTING RATING

	0.5	1	1.5	2	2.5	3	3.5	4	4.5	5
APPEARANCE										
AROMA										
FLAVOR										

	0.5	1	1.5	2	2.5	3	3.5	4	4.5	5
SWEET										
ACIDIC										
SPICY										
CITRUS										
CHOCOLATE										
CARAMEL										
BITTER										
SAVORY										

BREW METHOD

DRIP ☐ ESPRESSO ☐ PRESS ☐

POUR-OVER ☐ SIPHON ☐ OTHER ________

NOTES ______________________

RECOMMEND TO ______________________

COFFEE NAME ______________________ DATE ____________

BEVERAGE ______________________

PLACE TASTED ______________________ PRICE ____________

COUNTRY / REGION ______________________

COMPANY ______________________

TESTING RATING

	0.5	1	1.5	2	2.5	3	3.5	4	4.5	5
APPEARANCE										
AROMA										
FLAVOR										

	0.5	1	1.5	2	2.5	3	3.5	4	4.5	5
SWEET										
ACIDIC										
SPICY										
CITRUS										
CHOCOLATE										
CARAMEL										
BITTER										
SAVORY										

BREW METHOD

DRIP ☐ ESPRESSO ☐ PRESS ☐

POUR-OVER ☐ SIPHON ☐ OTHER ________

NOTES ______________________

RECOMMEND TO ______________________

COFFEE NAME ______________________ DATE ____________

BEVERAGE ______________________

PLACE TASTED ______________________ PRICE ____________

COUNTRY / REGION ______________________

COMPANY ______________________

TESTING RATING

	0.5	1	1.5	2	2.5	3	3.5	4	4.5	5
APPEARANCE										
AROMA										
FLAVOR										

	0.5	1	1.5	2	2.5	3	3.5	4	4.5	5
SWEET										
ACIDIC										
SPICY										
CITRUS										
CHOCOLATE										
CARAMEL										
BITTER										
SAVORY										

BREW METHOD

DRIP ☐ ESPRESSO ☐ PRESS ☐

POUR-OVER ☐ SIPHON ☐ OTHER ________

NOTES

____

RECOMMEND TO

____

COFFEE NAME ____________ DATE ____________

BEVERAGE ____________

PLACE TASTED ____________ PRICE ____________

COUNTRY / REGION ____________

COMPANY ____________

TESTING RATING

	0.5	1	1.5	2	2.5	3	3.5	4	4.5	5
APPEARANCE										
AROMA										
FLAVOR										

	0.5	1	1.5	2	2.5	3	3.5	4	4.5	5
SWEET										
ACIDIC										
SPICY										
CITRUS										
CHOCOLATE										
CARAMEL										
BITTER										
SAVORY										

BREW METHOD

DRIP ☐ ESPRESSO ☐ PRESS ☐

POUR-OVER ☐ SIPHON ☐ OTHER ____

NOTES ____________

RECOMMEND TO ____________

COFFEE NAME ______________________ DATE ____________

BEVERAGE ______________________

PLACE TASTED ______________________ PRICE ____________

COUNTRY / REGION ______________________

COMPANY ______________________

TESTING RATING

	0.5	1	1.5	2	2.5	3	3.5	4	4.5	5
APPEARANCE										
AROMA										
FLAVOR										

	0.5	1	1.5	2	2.5	3	3.5	4	4.5	5
SWEET										
ACIDIC										
SPICY										
CITRUS										
CHOCOLATE										
CARAMEL										
BITTER										
SAVORY										

BREW METHOD

DRIP ☐ ESPRESSO ☐ PRESS ☐

POUR-OVER ☐ SIPHON ☐ OTHER ________

NOTES

____

RECOMMEND TO

____

COFFEE NAME ______________________ DATE ____________

BEVERAGE ______________________

PLACE TASTED ______________________ PRICE ____________

COUNTRY / REGION ______________________

COMPANY ______________________

TESTING RATING

	0.5	1	1.5	2	2.5	3	3.5	4	4.5	5
APPEARANCE										
AROMA										
FLAVOR										

	0.5	1	1.5	2	2.5	3	3.5	4	4.5	5
SWEET										
ACIDIC										
SPICY										
CITRUS										
CHOCOLATE										
CARAMEL										
BITTER										
SAVORY										

BREW METHOD

DRIP ☐ ESPRESSO ☐ PRESS ☐

POUR-OVER ☐ SIPHON ☐ OTHER ________

NOTES ______________________

RECOMMEND TO ______________________

COFFEE NAME ______________________ DATE ____________

BEVERAGE ______________________

PLACE TASTED ______________________ PRICE ____________

COUNTRY / REGION ______________________

COMPANY ______________________

TESTING RATING

	0.5	1	1.5	2	2.5	3	3.5	4	4.5	5
APPEARANCE										
AROMA										
FLAVOR										

	0.5	1	1.5	2	2.5	3	3.5	4	4.5	5
SWEET										
ACIDIC										
SPICY										
CITRUS										
CHOCOLATE										
CARAMEL										
BITTER										
SAVORY										

BREW METHOD

DRIP ☐ ESPRESSO ☐ PRESS ☐

POUR-OVER ☐ SIPHON ☐ OTHER ________

NOTES

RECOMMEND TO

COFFEE NAME ______________________ DATE ____________

BEVERAGE ______________________

PLACE TASTED ______________________ PRICE ____________

COUNTRY / REGION ________________

COMPANY ______________________

TESTING RATING

	0.5	1	1.5	2	2.5	3	3.5	4	4.5	5
APPEARANCE										
AROMA										
FLAVOR										

	0.5	1	1.5	2	2.5	3	3.5	4	4.5	5
SWEET										
ACIDIC										
SPICY										
CITRUS										
CHOCOLATE										
CARAMEL										
BITTER										
SAVORY										

BREW METHOD

DRIP ☐ ESPRESSO ☐ PRESS ☐

POUR-OVER ☐ SIPHON ☐ OTHER ________

NOTES ______________________

RECOMMEND TO ______________________

COFFEE NAME ______________________ DATE ____________

BEVERAGE ______________________

PLACE TASTED ______________________ PRICE ____________

COUNTRY / REGION ______________________

COMPANY ______________________

TESTING RATING

	0.5	1	1.5	2	2.5	3	3.5	4	4.5	5
APPEARANCE										
AROMA										
FLAVOR										

	0.5	1	1.5	2	2.5	3	3.5	4	4.5	5
SWEET										
ACIDIC										
SPICY										
CITRUS										
CHOCOLATE										
CARAMEL										
BITTER										
SAVORY										

BREW METHOD

DRIP ☐ ESPRESSO ☐ PRESS ☐

POUR-OVER ☐ SIPHON ☐ OTHER ________

NOTES

RECOMMEND TO

COFFEE NAME ________________ DATE ________

BEVERAGE ________________

PLACE TASTED ________________ PRICE ________

COUNTRY / REGION ________________

COMPANY ________________

TESTING RATING

	0.5	1	1.5	2	2.5	3	3.5	4	4.5	5
APPEARANCE										
AROMA										
FLAVOR										

	0.5	1	1.5	2	2.5	3	3.5	4	4.5	5
SWEET										
ACIDIC										
SPICY										
CITRUS										
CHOCOLATE										
CARAMEL										
BITTER										
SAVORY										

BREW METHOD

DRIP ☐ ESPRESSO ☐ PRESS ☐

POUR-OVER ☐ SIPHON ☐ OTHER ________

NOTES ________________

RECOMMEND TO ________________

COFFEE NAME ______________________ DATE ____________

BEVERAGE ______________________

PLACE TASTED ______________________ PRICE ____________

COUNTRY / REGION ______________________

COMPANY ______________________

TESTING RATING

	0.5	1	1.5	2	2.5	3	3.5	4	4.5	5
APPEARANCE										
AROMA										
FLAVOR										

	0.5	1	1.5	2	2.5	3	3.5	4	4.5	5
SWEET										
ACIDIC										
SPICY										
CITRUS										
CHOCOLATE										
CARAMEL										
BITTER										
SAVORY										

BREW METHOD

DRIP ☐ ESPRESSO ☐ PRESS ☐

POUR-OVER ☐ SIPHON ☐ OTHER ________

NOTES ______________________

RECOMMEND TO ______________________

COFFEE NAME ____________________ DATE ____________

BEVERAGE ____________________

PLACE TASTED ____________________ PRICE ____________

COUNTRY / REGION ____________________

COMPANY ____________________

TESTING RATING

	0.5	1	1.5	2	2.5	3	3.5	4	4.5	5
APPEARANCE										
AROMA										
FLAVOR										

	0.5	1	1.5	2	2.5	3	3.5	4	4.5	5
SWEET										
ACIDIC										
SPICY										
CITRUS										
CHOCOLATE										
CARAMEL										
BITTER										
SAVORY										

BREW METHOD

DRIP ☐ ESPRESSO ☐ PRESS ☐

POUR-OVER ☐ SIPHON ☐ OTHER ________

NOTES ____________________

RECOMMEND TO ____________________

COFFEE NAME ____________________ DATE ____________

BEVERAGE ____________________

PLACE TASTED ____________________ PRICE ____________

COUNTRY / REGION ____________________

COMPANY ____________________

TESTING RATING

	0.5	1	1.5	2	2.5	3	3.5	4	4.5	5
APPEARANCE										
AROMA										
FLAVOR										

	0.5	1	1.5	2	2.5	3	3.5	4	4.5	5
SWEET										
ACIDIC										
SPICY										
CITRUS										
CHOCOLATE										
CARAMEL										
BITTER										
SAVORY										

BREW METHOD

DRIP ☐ ESPRESSO ☐ PRESS ☐

POUR-OVER ☐ SIPHON ☐ OTHER ________

NOTES ____________________

RECOMMEND TO ____________________

COFFEE NAME ______________________ DATE __________

BEVERAGE ______________________

PLACE TASTED ______________________ PRICE __________

COUNTRY / REGION ______________________

COMPANY ______________________

TESTING RATING

	0.5	1	1.5	2	2.5	3	3.5	4	4.5	5
APPEARANCE										
AROMA										
FLAVOR										

	0.5	1	1.5	2	2.5	3	3.5	4	4.5	5
SWEET										
ACIDIC										
SPICY										
CITRUS										
CHOCOLATE										
CARAMEL										
BITTER										
SAVORY										

BREW METHOD

DRIP ☐ ESPRESSO ☐ PRESS ☐

POUR-OVER ☐ SIPHON ☐ OTHER ______

NOTES

____

RECOMMEND TO

____

COFFEE NAME ______________________ DATE ____________

BEVERAGE ______________________

PLACE TASTED ______________________ PRICE ____________

COUNTRY / REGION ______________________

COMPANY ______________________

TESTING RATING

	0.5	1	1.5	2	2.5	3	3.5	4	4.5	5
APPEARANCE										
AROMA										
FLAVOR										

	0.5	1	1.5	2	2.5	3	3.5	4	4.5	5
SWEET										
ACIDIC										
SPICY										
CITRUS										
CHOCOLATE										
CARAMEL										
BITTER										
SAVORY										

BREW METHOD

DRIP ☐ ESPRESSO ☐ PRESS ☐

POUR-OVER ☐ SIPHON ☐ OTHER ________

NOTES ______________________

RECOMMEND TO ______________________

COFFEE NAME ______________________ DATE ____________

BEVERAGE ______________________

PLACE TASTED ______________________ PRICE ____________

COUNTRY / REGION ______________________

COMPANY ______________________

TESTING RATING

	0.5	1	1.5	2	2.5	3	3.5	4	4.5	5
APPEARANCE										
AROMA										
FLAVOR										

	0.5	1	1.5	2	2.5	3	3.5	4	4.5	5
SWEET										
ACIDIC										
SPICY										
CITRUS										
CHOCOLATE										
CARAMEL										
BITTER										
SAVORY										

BREW METHOD

DRIP ☐ ESPRESSO ☐ PRESS ☐

POUR-OVER ☐ SIPHON ☐ OTHER ________

NOTES ______________________

RECOMMEND TO ______________________

COFFEE NAME ______________________ DATE ____________

BEVERAGE ______________________

PLACE TASTED ______________________ PRICE ____________

COUNTRY / REGION ______________________

COMPANY ______________________

TESTING RATING

	0.5	1	1.5	2	2.5	3	3.5	4	4.5	5
APPEARANCE										
AROMA										
FLAVOR										

	0.5	1	1.5	2	2.5	3	3.5	4	4.5	5
SWEET										
ACIDIC										
SPICY										
CITRUS										
CHOCOLATE										
CARAMEL										
BITTER										
SAVORY										

BREW METHOD

DRIP ☐ ESPRESSO ☐ PRESS ☐

POUR-OVER ☐ SIPHON ☐ OTHER ________

NOTES ______________________

RECOMMEND TO ______________________

COFFEE NAME ______________________ DATE ____________

BEVERAGE ______________________

PLACE TASTED ______________________ PRICE ____________

COUNTRY / REGION ______________________

COMPANY ______________________

TESTING RATING

	0.5	1	1.5	2	2.5	3	3.5	4	4.5	5
APPEARANCE										
AROMA										
FLAVOR										

	0.5	1	1.5	2	2.5	3	3.5	4	4.5	5
SWEET										
ACIDIC										
SPICY										
CITRUS										
CHOCOLATE										
CARAMEL										
BITTER										
SAVORY										

BREW METHOD

DRIP ☐ ESPRESSO ☐ PRESS ☐

POUR-OVER ☐ SIPHON ☐ OTHER ________

NOTES ______________________

RECOMMEND TO ______________________

COFFEE NAME ______________________ DATE ____________

BEVERAGE ______________________

PLACE TASTED ______________________ PRICE ____________

COUNTRY / REGION ______________________

COMPANY ______________________

TESTING RATING

	0.5	1	1.5	2	2.5	3	3.5	4	4.5	5
APPEARANCE										
AROMA										
FLAVOR										

	0.5	1	1.5	2	2.5	3	3.5	4	4.5	5
SWEET										
ACIDIC										
SPICY										
CITRUS										
CHOCOLATE										
CARAMEL										
BITTER										
SAVORY										

BREW METHOD

DRIP ☐ ESPRESSO ☐ PRESS ☐

POUR-OVER ☐ SIPHON ☐ OTHER ________

NOTES ______________________

RECOMMEND TO ______________________

COFFEE NAME ____________________ DATE ____________

BEVERAGE ____________________

PLACE TASTED ____________________ PRICE ____________

COUNTRY / REGION ____________________

COMPANY ____________________

TESTING RATING

	0.5	1	1.5	2	2.5	3	3.5	4	4.5	5
APPEARANCE										
AROMA										
FLAVOR										

	0.5	1	1.5	2	2.5	3	3.5	4	4.5	5
SWEET										
ACIDIC										
SPICY										
CITRUS										
CHOCOLATE										
CARAMEL										
BITTER										
SAVORY										

BREW METHOD

DRIP ☐ ESPRESSO ☐ PRESS ☐

POUR-OVER ☐ SIPHON ☐ OTHER ________

NOTES

RECOMMEND TO

COFFEE NAME ____________________ DATE ____________

BEVERAGE ____________________

PLACE TASTED ____________________ PRICE ____________

COUNTRY / REGION ____________________

COMPANY ____________________

TESTING RATING

	0.5	1	1.5	2	2.5	3	3.5	4	4.5	5
APPEARANCE										
AROMA										
FLAVOR										

	0.5	1	1.5	2	2.5	3	3.5	4	4.5	5
SWEET										
ACIDIC										
SPICY										
CITRUS										
CHOCOLATE										
CARAMEL										
BITTER										
SAVORY										

BREW METHOD

DRIP ☐ ESPRESSO ☐ PRESS ☐

POUR-OVER ☐ SIPHON ☐ OTHER ________

NOTES

RECOMMEND TO

COFFEE NAME ____________ DATE ____________

BEVERAGE ____________

PLACE TASTED ____________ PRICE ____________

COUNTRY / REGION ____________

COMPANY ____________

TESTING RATING

	0.5	1	1.5	2	2.5	3	3.5	4	4.5	5
APPEARANCE										
AROMA										
FLAVOR										

	0.5	1	1.5	2	2.5	3	3.5	4	4.5	5
SWEET										
ACIDIC										
SPICY										
CITRUS										
CHOCOLATE										
CARAMEL										
BITTER										
SAVORY										

BREW METHOD

DRIP ☐ ESPRESSO ☐ PRESS ☐

POUR-OVER ☐ SIPHON ☐ OTHER ____________

NOTES ____________

RECOMMEND TO ____________

COFFEE NAME ______________________ DATE ____________

BEVERAGE ______________________

PLACE TASTED ______________________ PRICE ____________

COUNTRY / REGION ______________________

COMPANY ______________________

TESTING RATING

	0.5	1	1.5	2	2.5	3	3.5	4	4.5	5
APPEARANCE										
AROMA										
FLAVOR										

	0.5	1	1.5	2	2.5	3	3.5	4	4.5	5
SWEET										
ACIDIC										
SPICY										
CITRUS										
CHOCOLATE										
CARAMEL										
BITTER										
SAVORY										

BREW METHOD

DRIP ☐ ESPRESSO ☐ PRESS ☐

POUR-OVER ☐ SIPHON ☐ OTHER ________

NOTES ______________________

RECOMMEND TO ______________________

Printed in Great Britain
by Amazon

56196370R00071